The Unplanned Pregnancy Handbook

*Information, Resources and Real Life Stories
to Help YOU!*

Dorrie Williams-Wheeler

PublishAmerica

Baltimore

First printing

ISBN: 1-59286-014-1
PUBLISHED BY PUBLISHAMERICA BOOK
PUBLISHERS
www.publishamerica.com
Baltimore

Printed in the United States of America

Dedication

This book is dedicated to my biggest fan, my daddy Tommie Lee Williams. It is also dedicated to my husband Craig and my mother Marietta. Although they support me, they never took the time to read my books or scripts. Hopefully, that is all about to change.

Acknowledgements

I would like to thank all of the women who shared their stories with me to make this book possible. Whether they met with me in person or shared their stories via fax, phone or e-mail this book would not have been possible without them. I would like to thank the Hope Clinic in Granite City, Illinois for making their services available to the women of Southern Illinois and St. Louis. Without them many young women would be in a bind. You all have helped thousands. I would like to thank all of the Crisis Pregnancy Centers worldwide for all of the loving support they provide women who continue their pregnancies. Your services are invaluable and you all are a wonderful resource for young women in need. I would like to thank all of the maternity shelters employees who took the time to let me tour their facilities and who also provided me insight as to the services they perform. I would especially like to thank Eugenia Brown for her insight as to the functions and programs that maternity shelters offer. I would also like to thank my publisher, Publish America, for making this book—that will help so many women— possible.

Table of Contents

Foreword

Pregnancy can be one of the happiest times in a woman's life, but when that pregnancy is unplanned it can be a very tumultuous and trying time in a woman's life. Every year 48% of pregnancies among American women are unplanned. An unplanned pregnancy is one that is not wanted at all or is mistimed.

Every woman will deal with the knowledge of an unplanned pregnancy in their own method. Depending on their stage in life and various other factors, this will determine the outcome of the unplanned pregnancy. She may consult with the father of the child, her family or friends. Depending on the woman's age, she may need to enlist the assistance of her parents when resolving her impending pregnancy. Some women will keep this knowledge to themselves and resolve the situation in silence. Ultimately, how to deal with an unplanned pregnancy should be the woman's decision.

The Unplanned Pregnancy Handbook is not a pro-life or pro-choice book. This is a book intended to provide women in desperate situations with knowledge about all of the options they have available to them when grappling with an unplanned pregnancy.

The information in this book should not be substituted for advice from an actual physician. This book is only meant to provide information and guidance to woman facing a desperate situation.

This book also features real life stories of women who have been faced with unplanned pregnancies. All of the stories are true and only the names and locations have been changed.

Unplanned pregnancies occur for women of all ages. However,

many times it is the younger women who don't have the knowledge to educate themselves about their situation. Each year almost one million teenage women become pregnant, and of those one million, 78% of the teen pregnancies are unplanned. Sexually active teens who do not use any form of contraception have a 90% chance of becoming pregnant within one year.

Knowledge is power. I hope that this book will give women faced with unplanned pregnancies the strength to help themselves. This book can help the thousands of women who need answers to the questions that they are having.

If this book is helpful to you when you are in a desperate situation, pass it on to a friend when you are finished with it.

CHAPTER 1 - You Think You're Pregnant

DETERMINING THAT YOU ARE PREGNANT

Once you suspect that you are pregnant you must confirm this information. The first sign of a possible pregnancy for many women is a late period. Another sign of early pregnancy is nausea and vomiting. Some women may feel tenderness in their breast. Although these early symptoms may indicate pregnancy, just because you may experience one, none, or all of these symptoms, it is still important to take a pregnancy test.

If you suspect that you may be pregnant, you can purchase a home pregnancy test from your local drug store. Home pregnancy tests range in price from $7-$18 dollars. Home pregnancy tests look for a hormone named hCG in your urine. The presence of hCG is a strong indication of pregnancy. This hormone is produced by the placenta when a woman is pregnant. hCG can be detected in blood and urine as early as six days after fertilization has taken place.

If you are a minor, you don't need your parents' permission to purchase a home pregnancy test. The test can be taken in the privacy of your home. Many women prefer to take a home pregnancy test to confirm their pregnancy before they actually go see a doctor.

Some test can be taken as early as a few days before your period is actually late. However, the tests are more accurate when you take them close to the actual date of your period or shortly after your period is late.

If you do not feel comfortable administering the test to yourself, because you feel you may do the test wrong or for other reasons, there are many facilities that offer pregnancy testing.

MAKING YOUR DECISION

Pregnancy lasts approximately 280 days. If you find out that you are pregnant 4 weeks after your last menstrual cycle, you are already considered to be 4 weeks pregnant. This is important information for several reasons. One, if you are planning on continuing your pregnancy, you will need to make arrangements to see a doctor for pre-natal care. If this pregnancy was unplanned you may not have the necessary insurance for prenatal care and you may need to make arrangements to obtain medical insurance.

If you are considering terminating your pregnancy you need to plan accordingly. First trimester abortions are most common and have the least complications. They are also far less expensive than second trimester abortions. Therefore, if you are planning to have an abortion, you will need to find out how far along you are in your pregnancy. After you determine how far along you are in your pregnancy, you will need to find an abortion provider in your area. Once you find an abortion provider you will need to find out how much the procedure will cost.

Think hard about your options. You may decide to seek counseling before you actually decide how you are going to proceed. You may wish to discuss this information with your husband or boyfriend. Take time to think about your unplanned pregnancy, but don't take too much time. Time is of the essence and the sooner you make your decision the sooner you can proceed with your course of action.

CHAPTER 2 - Keeping Your Baby - The Long Road Ahead

SEEING A DOCTOR

Once you suspect that you may be pregnant, it is a good idea to schedule an appointment to see a doctor. If you do not have an obstetrician/gynecologist, you can schedule your initial visit with your family doctor or a general practitioner. The doctor will then confirm your pregnancy and refer you to an OB/GYN for prenatal care. Confirming your pregnancy is important, because although rare, sometimes home pregnancy tests can be wrong. Also many women fear they may be pregnant because their period has stopped or is late, and often pregnancy is not the cause for this problem.

PRENATAL CARE

If you have decided to continue your pregnancy to term, prenatal care is vital for both you and your baby. If you do not have insurance, there are programs that will assist you in obtaining insurance and/or free or reduced prenatal care.

During your first and second trimester you will visit your doctor once a month for prenatal care. Starting at 30 weeks, during your third trimester, you may begin seeing your doctor every two weeks. During your ninth month, starting at 36 weeks, you may begin seeing your doctor once a week. If your pregnancy is considered high risk you may see your doctor more often throughout the duration of your pregnancy.

Prenatal care consists of monitoring and testing you and the baby. During the first visit you will be asked about previous pregnancies, whether you smoke, drink or take any drugs, and about the family medical history of you and your partner.

During routine visits you will be subject to various tests. At most routine visits you will be weighed, given a urine screening, and have your blood pressure taken. Your doctor will listen to fetal heart tones with a Doppler, and may ask you general questions about your health.

Below are tests that you may be given during your prenatal care. Please keep in mind that every prenatal care facility is different and you may not be given all of the test mentioned. Your doctor will make sure that you get the best prenatal care that you need to have a happy and healthy pregnancy.

FIRST TRIMESTER TESTS

Pregnancy Test - You will be given a pregnancy test even if you took an over the counter test. The doctor must confirm your pregnancy.

Urine Test - The urine test looks for sugar and protein in your urine. Too much sugar can mean that your body is not processing sugar properly and protein in the urine can signal high blood pressure or a kidney problem. The urine test can also determine bladder and other urinary tract infections.

Blood Test - Usually at your first visit blood will be drawn. The blood tests determine your blood type and detect anemia and any infections the mother may have. The blood drawn may also be used for various screening exams, such as to see if the mother is a carrier for Sickle Cell Anemia. Your Rh type will also be determined. Rh type refers to the presence of positive or absence of negative Rh factor in your blood. Your Rh type is noted to look for Rh incompatibility between you and the fetus. Rh incompatibility occurs when a Rh negative mother produces an Rh positive child.

Culture of the Cervix and Vagina - The doctor performs this test to determine if you have certain diseases such as chlamydia, gonorrhea or other sexually transmitted diseases. These tests are important because these diseases can be potentially harmful to the fetus. If the cultures come back positive you will be treated.

Pap Smear - Even if you just had one, your doctor may perform a Pap Smear as part of your routine prenatal care. The Pap Smear tests for cervical cancer.

HIV Test - Some doctors offices give HIV test to pregnant women. Not all prenatal care facilities offer this test. You will be given the opportunity to sign a consent form and you can object to this test if do not feel it is necessary. If your test results are positive, you may be put on AZT or a similar drug to avoid potentially passing the HIV virus to your child.

SECOND TRIMESTER TESTS

Maternal Serum Alpha-Fetoprotein and Multiple Marker Screening - This test is usually given between 15-18 weeks of pregnancy. This test is performed by drawing a sample of blood. The test checks the levels of Alpha-Fetoprotein. Abnormal levels can indicate Downs Syndrome or Spina Bifida.

Ultrasound - An ultrasound is a test that uses sound waves to produce pictures of the fetus. Some physicians will perform a first trimester ultrasound which is known as a transvaginal ultrasound. A first trimester ultrasound can accurately date the pregnancy. A first trimester pregnancy can also ensure that the pregnancy is proceeding as it should. A second trimester ultrasound is usually given between 18-20 weeks. The second trimester ultrasound can verify your due date, detect malformations in the fetus, detect multiple pregnancies, or detect other complications, such as a low lying placenta. Another ultrasound may be offered during the third trimester to determine the position of the fetus. Often depending on your insurance plan or doctor, you may only have one ultrasound during your pregnancy or none at all. It really depends on your physician and insurance plan. An ultrasound is not performed in every pregnancy.

Amniocentesis - This test looks for birth defects in the fetus. This test is not always given in routine pregnancies. The test may be ordered if a woman has an abnormal Maternal Serum Alpha-Fetoprotein and Multiple Marker screening test result. Women over 35 or who have high risks pregnancies are almost always given this test. The test is preformed when the doctor puts a needle into the mothers uterus through her belly and draws amniotic fluid.

Glucose Screening - Glucose screening is another blood test. The mother is given a special sugary drink to ingest. Her blood is then drawn about an hour later to test the sugar levels in her blood. This test is usually given between 24-28 weeks.

THIRD TRIMESTER TESTS

Fetal Non Stress Test - A non stress test is an external test performed in high risk pregnancies during the third trimester. The test is performed by having the woman lie down and wear two belts. One of the belts monitors for contractions and the other belt monitors the fetal heart beat. The test is performed for various reasons including gestational diabetes, decreased fetal movement or if a woman has gone beyond her due date.

Group B Strep Test - Many healthy women carry Group B Strep bacteria, however, this bacteria can be harmful to newborns. Between 35-37 weeks the woman's vagina and rectum is swabbed and tested. If Group B Strep is present, the woman may be given antibiotics during delivery to protect the infant.

INSURANCE

Being a pregnant woman you are going to need insurance to cover your prenatal care and the birth of your child. Without insurance this type of medical treatment can be very costly. Between exams and tests your first prenatal visit can cost several hundred dollars.

If you are a minor and on your parents insurance, you should have your parents contact their insurance company to find out if they will cover prenatal care for a dependent. You should also find out if they will be able to add the baby to their insurance after the birth of the child.

If you are insured through your employment, college, or spouse it is always a good idea to call your insurance company and inform them of your pregnancy. Some insurance companies require that you have a referral to obtain OB/GYN care for prenatal services. Others do not require this step. It is also a good idea to know exactly what services are covered for your prenatal care. Whereas some insurance companies will allow a woman to get numerous ultrasounds throughout her pregnancy and allow every test under the sun to be performed, other insurance companies may only cover one ultrasound, whereas some may not pay for an ultrasound at all unless deemed medically necessary. Every insurance company is different so it is best that you know the ends and outs of your insurance company regarding your prenatal care.

Insurance companies only give you a certain amount of time after the birth of the child for you to enroll the child onto your insurance policy. Contact the insurance company immediately after the birth of your child. Your hospital bill for the child birth will be separate than the baby's medical bill, and if the child is not added onto an insurance plan you may have to pay for their portion of the bill.

PROGRAMS TO HELP YOU

You've just discovered that you are pregnant. You have no money, no job, no insurance and no stable home life. The above may or may not apply to you, but no matter how desperate your situation may seem there are many programs out there to help you continue your pregnancy if you desire to. Once you have the knowledge, you can proceed with your pregnancy with greater ease.

MEDICAID
Medicaid is a form of insurance for low income people. Medicaid was established under the Federal Social Security Act to allow states to provide medical assistance for individuals on public aid and also for low income individuals. If you have income coming into your household, yet do not have sufficient income for medical insurance, you may qualify for Medicaid assistance.

To apply for Medicaid you would contact your local Department of Health and Human Services Office. Some states call their Department of Health and Human Services-Social Services. Medicaid insurance will allow you to obtain necessary prenatal care and it will cover your child birth for you and your child.

FOOD STAMPS
The Food Stamp program is a program sponsored by the US Department of Agriculture. The Food Stamp Program provides benefits to low income households. Depending on your state, a food stamp recipient will receive actual food stamp coupons that can be used at grocery stores to purchase food items or they may be issued an EBT card. The EBT, which is short for Electronic Benefits Transfer Card, puts a food stamp recipients benefits on an electronic debit card. Even if you do not qualify for TANF or Medicaid, you may

still qualify for The Food Stamp Program.

Based on your family size and income that is how it will be determined exactly how much you will receive monthly in food stamp benefits. It is possible to receive both Food Stamps and WIC assistance. To apply for Food Stamps contact your local social services or human services department. To find the nearest location in your area, The Food Stamp Program has a 24 hour toll free phone number. This is not a number that you can call to apply by phone for Food Stamp benefits. This number will only tell you where you can apply for Food Stamp benefits in your area. In addition to helping you locate the number to your nearest social services or health department, the hotline also provides pre-recorded nutrition information. The number was established in 1999. The toll-free Food Stamp information number is 1-800-221-5689.

THE WOMEN INFANT & CHILDREN PROGRAM (WIC)

The WIC program is a program developed to help the well being of low income women, infants and children under the age of 5. The WIC program provides nutritious food to women and children. The program also provides mothers with formula for their infants.

Many women are not aware of the WIC program. The WIC program is not as difficult to qualify for as the Food Stamp program. Therefore, if you are turned down for Food Stamps, you may be eligible to receive WIC benefits. Even a low income married woman and her children can qualify for WIC assistance. A pregnant woman can receive WIC benefits for herself during her pregnancy and for six months after the birth of her child. She can receive WIC benefits for herself for up to one year if she is breast feeding. A child can remain on the WIC program up until the age of 5. WIC serves 45% of the infants born in the United States.

In addition to providing nutritious foods to women and children, the WIC program also provides women with nutrition information, health screening for herself and her children and referrals to other welfare agencies.

The way that WIC works, is that a woman on the program is

given WIC checks or vouchers that she can take to a special WIC store or to her local grocery store. The vouchers specify the items that can be purchased. Once the woman has shopped for the items on the voucher, she would turn in the WIC voucher to the cashier when checking out of the store. WIC foods include infant formula and cereals, cheese, milk, eggs, and adult cereals. Depending on the woman's profile, she may qualify for other WIC items such as peanut butter, beans, carrots and tuna. When you enroll in the program they will tell you what items you may purchase.

To find out about your local WIC program, contact your local health department.

WELFARE:
TEMPORARY ASSISTANCE FOR NEEDY FAMILIES

Depending on your financial situation, you may qualify for TANF. TANF is short for Temporary Assistance For Needy Families, which some people simply refer to as welfare benefits. TANF provides limited assistance to needy families with children to promote work, responsibility and self-sufficiency. TANF provides cash benefits for recipients. The amount of your cash benefits will be determined by the size of your family and other factors, such as if there is other income coming into the home.

If you receive TANF you may automatically qualify for Medicaid and or the Food Stamp program. To apply for TANF, you will need to fill out an application available from your local department of social services. The work component of TANF requires recipients to be working or actively seeking employment. It is meant to be a temporary assistance program. States determine which services/ benefits to provide and whom to serve. Cash grants, work opportunities, and other services are provided directly to needy families.

CRISIS PREGNANCY CENTERS

Crisis Pregnancy Centers are facilities that help women who have decided to continue with their pregnancy whether she has decided to place her child up for adoption or if she plans to raise the child on her own. If a woman is considering an abortion, she should not go to a Crisis Pregnancy Center because even though they will provide some abortion information, they are far more helpful in helping pregnant women who wish to carry their pregnancy to term than those who plan to abort. They provide women with abortion alternatives.

For the woman facing an unplanned pregnancy who has decided to proceed with her pregnancy, a Crisis Pregnancy Center can be a wonderful resource and help her in more ways than she could ever imagine.

Crisis Pregnancy Centers provide free services to pregnant women. They offer free pregnancy tests and a wide range of other services. All services are confidential. The people who work at Crisis Pregnancy Centers can offer you a loving shoulder to cry on and can also be strong for you when you feel that you can't carry on. The centers offer counseling services and if a woman needs one, they can have a personal advocate who will work with them throughout their pregnancy.

Education is a big part of the role of the Crisis Pregnancy Center. The centers often have guest speakers and they have a collection of books and videos about pregnancy and fetal development.

The Centers also provide referrals for housing, adoption, medical assistance, maternity and infant clothing and equipment. Some Crisis Pregnancy Centers even hold baby showers for the women who attend classes at the centers. Classes offered at some of the centers include nutrition, infant CPR, parenting skills, and breast feeding.

MATERNITY SHELTERS

You never know if you will find yourself in a situation where housing may become an issue. If you find yourself in need of shelter, there are places that can help you. Pregnant teens may find themselves with no place to go and need to utilize the resources of a maternity shelter. A woman in an abusive relationship who doesn't have the financial means to get away, but wants to leave the relationship for the safety of herself and her unborn child may utilize the services of a maternity shelter. A college student who wants to continue her education, but her university doesn't offer family housing. The situation may vary, but the services of these shelters are invaluable.

There are maternity shelters for teens and adult women in all 50 states. The services offered and the age range of clients accepted varies from shelter to shelter. Some of the services offered by the shelters include:

Safe short term housing-sometimes up to two years
Educational assistance
Parenting classes
Substance abuse counseling
Daycare assistance
Job training and placement assistance
Clothing for the mother and the children
Outreach services
Independent living skills

If you are in need of a maternity shelter, they are there and it is best to call several shelters to find one that is best for you. Whereas some shelters only service teens, other service woman of all ages. Many of the shelters have rules that you may find unacceptable, such as curfews or no overnight passes, so it is best that you find a shelter that would work best for your situation. Some shelters also limit the number of children that a client may have, and have restrictions on age limits. Most shelters have limited bed space, so you may have to call around.

Lifecall is a web site dedicated to educating teens and helping pregnant women. They have an on-line directory of maternity shelters, organized state by state. The URL of the Lifecall web site can be found in the web resources section of this book.

MATERNITY LEAVE
Maternity leave is the name given to the time off a woman takes

from work after giving birth. It usually ranges from 4-6 weeks. However, if you make special arrangements with your employer, or have complications with your pregnancy, you can arrange to take a longer maternity leave.

If you work full time, your employer most likely will offer you up to six weeks for maternity leave to take care of your newborn child. Don't make the mistake and assume that you automatically get maternity leave. Small companies and certain other types of employers do not have to comply with maternity leave laws. If the company that you work for employs more than 15 people, you cannot be fired if you go on maternity leave. You are protected under the same laws that protect disabled employees. Talk to your employer. This is the best way to find out the options available to you.

Some jobs offer employees a paid 6 week maternity leave. Others may offer employees 50% of their current pay while they are on maternity leave. Some jobs don't offer any kind of financial support towards maternity leave and require that employees use their sick time or vacation time. If you do not have enough sick or vacation time you may have to return to work or continue to take time off in a leave without pay status. Communication is the key. Contact your supervisor or human resources department at least several months prior to your delivery.

Some women can't afford to take the time off for maternity leave, but they will need to in order to bond with their new child and to allow their body time to heal. In rare cases, women will return to work immediately after giving birth.

Most jobs don't want you at work immediately after giving birth. Some jobs require a doctors release before allowing you to return to work.

If your job does not offer a paid maternity leave, and you don't have enough vacation or sick leave to cover your maternity leave, try to discuss other options with your employer. Your company may have a leave sharing program that will allow other employees to donate some of their vacation time to you. Your employer may also allow you to telecommute or work from home during your maternity leave to allow you to keep generating income during your time off.

MATERNITY LEAVE STORIES

Lacy

"I was working as a waitress when I had my daughter. I went into labor on Thursday morning, was released from the hospital Friday, and was back at work Saturday night. People kept trying to scare me and tell me that I would hemorrhage or bleed too much from standing on my feet all day and that my body had to heal. They didn't understand my situation. I was a single parent living in a pay by the week hotel and I had to pay for diapers. My co-workers babysat for free while I worked."

Portia

"I had a corporate job. The insurance was excellent, but I had only been on the job for 5 months before I needed to take time off for maternity leave. I only had 14 hours of vacation time and 8 hours of sick leave. I had been sick during my pregnancy and had to use some of the leave I had been accruing. My company didn't allow women to return to work after having a child until six weeks had passed and they had a doctor's release. It sucked. The little money I did have I had to use to pay the premium to keep my health insurance going. If it wasn't for my husband I don't know how I would have made it. It was tough trying to make it on one income for those six weeks, but it had to be done."

Holly

"I was working as a legal secretary for a law firm that had three attorneys. By law, they didn't have to comply with any maternity leave laws, but they tried to accommodate me. They hired a temp who was completely lost and called me at home every day. During my time out, they went through 4 temps, who all became overwhelmed and quit. I was running out of money because I only had two weeks of vacation time saved up. I returned to work 3 ½ weeks after having my baby. I needed the job. They said they weren't going to fire me, but they called me at home so much and sounded so frustrated I felt like my job was on the line."

The Family And Medical Leave Act

The Family and Medical Leave Act, passed in 1993, requires employers to provide up to 12 weeks of unpaid leave in cases of personal illness, illnesses of parents, spouses or children and childbirth.

This law does not apply to everyone or every situation. Companies that employee 50 employees or less do not have to comply. In addition, the person wishing to utilize the benefits of the Family and Medical Leave Act has to have been on the job at least 1 year.

The Family Medical Leave Act will protect your job for up to 12 weeks and it will insure that your health benefits will not be canceled-although you may have to pay insurance premiums.

This law is complex and it is important that you understand the procedures for applying for this leave and all of the ends and outs. Talk to your employer or human resources department if you are interested in pursuing the Family and Medical Leave Act.

CHILDCARE

If you work or go to school, you will need someone to care for your child when you are away. It is important to plan your child care in advance. Daycare centers often have long waiting lists for infants, therefore it is best to start calling around before your ninth month. If you plan on having a relative or friend care for you baby, make arrangements to sit down and talk to them beforehand. Determine how you will compensate them for their time.

If you do decide to pay a friend or family member to care for your child, purchase a receipt book and keep accurate records of the amount of money you pay them for child care. Also, you will need their social security number in order to file your taxes properly and to receive a child care credit.

Daycare Centers

Daycare centers provide child care to small children. Day care providers will nurture your child, and as your child grows he or she will have an opportunity to interact with other children.

Traditional day care centers are usually operate between 6AM and 7PM. If you work or go to school in the evenings or on weekends, a traditional day care may not be the ideal child care option for you. Daycare centers are rather expensive. Infant care prices can range from $100-$300 a week depending on the area you live in and the type of daycare center you choose for your child.

Most day care centers begin taking infants at six weeks of age. The majority of day care centers require parents to provide diapers, formula or expressed breast milk and wipes for their infants.

When choosing a day care center make sure that the facility is licensed and that they require background checks on all of their employees. Investigate any prospective day care center. Ask friends and neighbors if they have heard anything about the facility or if they had positive or negative experiences with the facility.

Don't rush to judgement when choosing a day care. Don't choose a facility based on how large their ad is in the phone book or because they always have commercials on television. Arrange to visit the day care prior to enrolling your child. Take a mental note of how the staff interacts with the infants. Also monitor safety conditions at the day care center. Does the front door have a buzzer? Are walkways clear?

Prior to enrolling your child, the day care center may ask you for a deposit to hold your spot. Often these deposits are non-refundable, so be sure of your decision before paying any type of deposit.

Before choosing to put your child in a traditional day care center, assess your situation. Will the operating hours of the day care center fit within your schedule? If your child becomes sick will you be able to find alternative child care? These are just a few of the questions you should ask yourself when trying to determine what type of child care situation is best for you.

Home Day Care

Licensed home based day care centers operate similar to traditional day care centers. They have to abide by certain rules regarding the number of children they can care for and their home is subject to inspection by the state. Home day care providers are required to follow strict standards regarding safety, training, nutrition, and the equipment in their homes.

One of the benefits of home day care centers is that they often offer more flexibility than traditional day care centers. Depending on the provider, they may offer evening and weekend child care. Sometimes home day care is less expensive that traditional day care.

Use the same skills that you would use when choosing a traditional day care center when you are looking for a home day care provider. You will need to ask a few more questions of home day care providers. Find out if there will be older children or other adults in the house in the same area where the children will be cared from. Also ensure that the provider has safe cribs for infants. If the provider doesn't have cribs or playpens for your child, you may have to provide these. Make sure that the area where the children are being cared for is safe.

FEEDING YOUR BABY

Breastfeeding

Breastfeeding is the easiest way to feed your new baby. It's cheaper than bottle feeding and it's convenient. The American Academy of Pediatrics determined that breast milk is the ideal nutrition for your babies first twelve months of life.

Some women are apprehensive about breast feeding due to things they have heard from families and friends. If you deliver your baby in a hospital, many hospitals have lactation consultants that can assist you with breastfeeding. If the hospital you deliver at has no lactation consultant available, a nurse may be able to help you with breastfeeding basics such as helping your baby latch on to your breast.

Even if you are going to be a working mom or a mom that goes to school, you can still choose to nurse your baby. Your breast milk can be expressed into a bottle by hand or with a breast pump.

The La Leche League International is an organization dedicated to providing information and support to women who choose to breast feed. You can look in your phone book or visit the La Leche League's web site to find a Le Leche League group in your area.

If there is no La Leche League in your area, your doctor, local health department or a Crisis Pregnancy Center may be able to assist your with breastfeeding basics.

Formula Feeding

Don't feel like a failure if breastfeeding is not for you. Millions of women formula feed their babies every year and they thrive and grow into healthy toddlers.

Formula Feeding may cost you up to $1200 a year. If you are on the WIC program, they will be able to provide you with infant formula for free. When choosing a formula, select an iron fortified formula. There are many different brands on the market, but they are similar. Choose one formula for your infant and only switch formula if your doctor suggests that your infant change formula.

Many of the popular infant formulas give out coupons and free samples. By visiting their web sites you can often sign up for their mailing lists.

AFTER THE BABY

After your baby is born you may find yourself overwhelmed. Now you will be the mother of a new little person who will depend on you for their every need. Whether this is your first child or a second or third, every new child will require your love and attention.

The birth of a new child can be a joyous and a stressful time.

If you find yourself feeling very sad and depressed after the birth of your child you may be developing postpartum depression. Postpartum depression refers to the mental state of a woman following the birth of a child. If you feel hopeless and extremely sad it is important that you contact your health care provider. This is a treatable condition.

STORIES OF UNPLANNED PREGNANCIES

Marisol - Age 19
My High School Sweetheart Broke My Heart

"My story is so painful for me to tell. Justin was my high school sweetheart. We dated all through high school. He was a year ahead of me, so when I was a junior he was a senior looking forward to graduation and college. He had a football scholarship and was going to college several states away. We planned to stay close through e-mail and holiday breaks. I never thought Justin and I would break up. I thought that we would be together forever. I was so naïve.

"Justin left for college in August the week before Labor Day. Soon after he left, I discovered that I was pregnant. Let me go back in time a little. As soon as he arrived at college, I didn't really hear from him anymore. He told me he was busy with school and football so I believed him. When I told him I was pregnant, he told me that I was lying and that it probably wasn't his because he had been gone almost a month.

"I became so sad and depressed. Justin never called or wrote. I called him constantly at his dorm room and his roommate always said that he wasn't there. I did consider having an abortion, but I didn't have any money and I was too embarrassed to tell my dad that I was pregnant. My mother had passed away several years earlier from cancer and my dad was doing his best to raise me and my brother.

"I managed to scrape up enough money to catch the Greyhound

bus to Ohio to visit Justin—a trip that took over a day and was hundreds of miles from my home in Minnesota. When I arrived at his dorm, he hung up the phone when I told him I was outside of his building.

I felt so damn stupid. I had bought a one way ticket and I had about $7 in my purse. I didn't have hotel money, I was 17 and pregnant and I just knew that when I saw Justin that he would have a change of heart.

"I sat outside of the dorm crying when I met some girls that went to Justin's school. If it wasn't for them I don't know what I would have done. They let me stay with them. Justin did finally agree to see me, but when we met in his dorm room, it was not good. We argued and he became violent. He slapped me and pushed me to the ground during a heated argument. I couldn't believe that he would hit me while I was pregnant. This wasn't the first time he had been violent, but for some reason I thought that me being pregnant would change things.

"The girls I met gave me money for a bus ticket and I went back home. I managed to tell my father that I was pregnant and he was supportive. I gave birth to a precious baby girl. Justin has only seen the baby through pictures. He is still in college, so I don't get any child support from him. I got on welfare and when I graduated from high school. I moved into a Section 8 apartment. I attend classes at the community college. I don't regret having my little girl. I do wish that Justin and I could be together as a couple. "

Keisha - Age 16
Someone Else To Think About

"My story is straight stupid. My baby's daddy is just a jerk. We hooked up when I was 15 and he was 17. He told me that his ex-girlfriend had aborted his baby and that is why they broke up. He told me that he would love to have a baby by me because I was pretty and light-skinned and that our baby would look so pretty. Why was I so dumb? I wasn't trying to get pregnant, but let's put it like this-I wasn't doing much to prevent it. We never used protection and when I became pregnant he was happy.

"When the baby came everything changed. He still wanted to hang out with his friends. He would drop off diapers and small amounts of money, but he never helped me take care of the baby. We would argue all the time and we broke up. He now has a new girlfriend-who is pregnant. He works at the grocery store and I get child support -$123 a month, which is not much at all, but I guess it's better than nothing. I love my daughter, and he loves her also. I definitely wish I would have waited. It is very, very hard to be a high school student and a mother. My family helps me, but I feel like I am missing out on a lot of things. Most of my friends have babies, but I always have to think about my daughter. I can't just think about Keisha anymore. It's tough."

Nadia - Age-22
He's The One Missing Out

"Grady and I had a strictly sexual relationship. We were both juniors in college. I knew he had a girlfriend out there in the world somewhere, but when he and I were together, our time together was really special. I can admit it, I was in love and I didn't take my pills on schedule because I felt like if I got pregnant by Grady everything would be alright.

"Well everything wasn't alright. It was winter time when I found out that I was pregnant. I told Grady and he snapped. He was angry, he said I was trying to mess up the good thing that we had, and that it probably wasn't his. He immediately cut off our relationship. He wouldn't take my calls and whenever I went to his dorm room his roommate said he wasn't there.

"My due date was in August. Grady went home for summer break in May and I was hoping that over the summer he would have an opportunity to think about things and he would come around. When school started, Grady was nowhere to be found. Much to my surprise, he transferred to a school 1000 miles away. Who would transfer during their senior year? That is how bad he wanted to not be a part of me or my child's life.

"I love my daughter. I finished college and started a teaching job the following year. Grady agreed to a paternity test after he was served him with child support papers and I now get child support. I love my daughter. He has never seen her, but he is the one missing out."

Kizzy - Age 23
Every Cloud Has A Silver Lining

"As a teenager I was always in and out of trouble. My parents weren't divorced, they were married, but they were both drug addicts. I lost my virginity at age 11 when I had sex with a man from my father's job who was living with us while he and his wife were having problems. When I was in high school, I never used drugs, but I did steal. I stole clothes from the mall, and money from fast food jobs I had worked. I was in and out of juvenile detention as a youth. I had many different sex partners, no less than 15 by the time I was 17 years old.

"By the time I was 19, I was living with some girlfriends. I was hooked on heroin and would sell things I stole to support my habit. One of my girlfriends died of a drug overdose that same year, so I decided to clean up my act.

"When I was 21, I was working doing telemarketing and living with my new boyfriend. Much to our surprise, I became pregnant. We had only been together three months. I went to my first prenatal visit and the doctor drew some blood for various tests. Much to my surprise, I got the biggest whammy surprise. Several weeks after the visit it was revealed that my HIV test came back positive. I was so depressed and my boyfriend was shocked and scared-but he didn't leave. I really considered abortion, but the doctor told me that if I took medication throughout my pregnancy there was a chance the baby would not be HIV positive. I became very depressed about being HIV positive. I don't know how I contracted the virus. I gave birth to a healthy 9 pound baby boy on my 22 birthday.

"Our son is HIV negative, however he will have to be tested regularly up until the age five. I went on to have another child, a daughter the next year. My boyfriend and I are still together and he is HIV negative. My children changed my life, and I am healthy and we are doing fine. I am frightened about being HIV positive, but I have learned that people can live very productive lives and be HIV positive."

Debbie - Age 19
A Bit Earlier Than We Planned, But It's Working

"Have you ever heard the story about the girl who lost her virginity on her prom night and got pregnant? Yeah, I bet you missed that one. That's what happened to me. My boyfriend and I had been together for four years and I promised him that we would go "all the way" on prom night.

"Our inexperience was a problem because the condom broke and he didn't even realize it. I didn't know about the morning-after pill, and I became pregnant. I was planning on going away to college and my boyfriend was planning on going to the Air Force.

"We changed our plans around big time. He still enlisted in the Air Force, but we got married much sooner than we had planned. We had always said that if our relationship survived 4 years of college that we would tie the knot. The military has good benefits and we live in military family housing. I enrolled in several college courses and our daughter goes to day care.

"I feel like such a grown-up now. I cook dinner, change diapers, and iron my husband's uniform. I feel sad sometimes when I talk to my friends from home and they are telling me about college parties and sororities and all the things I am missing out on, but I made this decision for myself and I have to live with it. Sometimes I wonder what would have happened if I would have had an abortion, but I love my family and I am glad that I chose this path for myself."

CHAPTER 3 - Abortion - No Easy Way Out

WHAT IS ABORTION?

Abortion is defined as the termination of a pregnancy. 50% of all unplanned pregnancies result in an abortion. The term induced abortion is used to describe any procedure that results in termination and expulsion of a fetus. Abortion became legal in the United States in January of 1973 when the United States Supreme Court handed down the Roe v. Wade decision allowing women to seek legal abortions. Abortion is a common procedure and many women choose abortion to end an unplanned pregnancy. An estimated 43% of women will have at least 1 abortion by the time they are 45 years old.

Any woman wishing to terminate her pregnancy before 24 weeks of gestation may seek an abortion in the United States. Pregnancy occurs in three stages. The first stage is known as the first trimester. The first trimester is considered between 1-12 weeks of pregnancy. The second stage of pregnancy is known as the second trimester. The second trimester ranges from 12-24 weeks of pregnancy. Abortions after 24 weeks of gestation are rare and uncommon unless the health of the mother is in danger.

Abortion is a relatively safe procedure. Many women fear that the procedure may be painful and lead to complications. Less than 1% of women who have abortions experience a major complication such as a pelvic infection. There are myths that women that have abortions will have problems conceiving in the future. This is not true. There is no evidence of childbearing problems among women who have had a vacuum aspiration abortion, the most common procedure, within the first 12 weeks of pregnancy.

GETTING AN ABORTION

Once a woman has determined that she is pregnant and wishes to seek an abortion she should act quickly to terminate her pregnancy. Abortions that take place during the first trimester have less complications and are less expensive than abortions that take place later in the pregnancy. 88% of women who seek abortions have them in the first 12 weeks of pregnancy.

Abortions usually take place in clinics, doctor's offices or hospital facilities. Depending on the type of area that you live in will determine the cost and availability of getting the procedure done. In many large urban areas, abortions are easy to come by. However, women that live in rural areas often have to travel hundreds of miles to obtain an abortion. Often when they reach the clinic, the cost may be much higher than the national average due to the fact that the clinic is the only one in the area that offers the procedure.

Once you have found a facility to perform the procedure, you should inquire about the cost of the procedure. In 1997, the cost of a non-hospital abortion with local anesthesia at 10 weeks of gestation ranged from $150 to $1,535, and the average amount paid was $316. The cost often depends on the area that you live in and the availability of other abortion providers in the area.

When you call for a quote, you will be asked how many weeks you are. If you can determine this on your own, they will provide a price quote. Before the procedure is done, most clinics will perform a vaginal scan ultrasound to properly date the pregnancy before the procedure is performed. 43% of all abortion facilities provide services only through the 12th week of pregnancy. If you find out that you are further along in your pregnancy than you calculated, you may have to re-consider your decision to have an abortion or find a facility that offers second trimester abortions.

INSURANCE AND OTHER PAYMENT METHODS

If you have insurance, your insurance provider may or may not pay for an induced abortion. It is best to ask the facility that is providing the procedure what type of insurance they accept. In addition, you should place a call to your insurance provider to make sure that your policy covers the procedure. If your insurance company does not cover the procedure you may have to pay cash for the procedure, or seek an alternative method of payment. Some states pay for abortions for women who cannot afford the procedure. 14% of abortions in this country are paid for by state funds.

It may also be wise to check with the facility to find out what type of payment methods they accept. Some abortion facilities do not accept checks, others only accept certain types of credit cards. Some facilities only accept money orders and don't take cash. This is why it is important to find out this valuable information before you make the trip. Often clinics base the procedure on the number of weeks you are vs. the trimester. So it may be wise to have extra money available if it is determined you are further along than you calculated.

PARENTAL CONSENT

There is much to consider before getting an abortion . If you are a minor, certain states have parental consent laws. These laws vary from state to state. Parental consent laws require minors to have parental permission before receiving an abortion. Other states require parental notification. This only requires that parents be notified. All states allow the minor the opportunity to go before a judge if they do not want to involve their parents. The specifics of the laws vary from state to state. When you contact the facility to schedule your procedure they can inform you of the laws in your particular state.

Below are the states that currently require parental consent or notification:

AL, AR, DE, GA, IA, ID, IN, KS, KY, LA, MA, MD, MI, MN, MO, MS, NC, ND, NE, OH, OK, PA, RI, SC, SD, TN, TX, UT, VA,WI, WV, and WY

MANDATORY WAITING PERIODS

Another obstacle facing women wishing to obtain an abortion is waiting periods. Waiting periods are legally enforced waiting periods that a women must adhere to before getting an abortion. Mandatory waiting periods for abortions came into effect in 1992 following the Supreme Court decision in Planned Parenthood of Southeastern Pennsylvania v. Casey. This ruling enforced a mandatory 25 hour waiting period before an abortion can be performed. Currently 15 states require waiting periods.

In many instances a woman will have to come into the clinic for a counseling session and she will be required to return in 18-24 hours to have the procedure performed. This ruling can cause more strain in an already strenuous situation. 86% of the counties in the United States where a third of American women of childbearing age live, have no doctors trained, qualified, and willing to perform abortions.

If a woman has to travel a great distance or even out of state to get an abortion, the mandatory waiting period will cause her to have to spend more money on a hotel room and related travel expenses.

This also can cause other difficulties. What if the woman has other children or a job that she can't get away from? Mandatory waiting periods may cause her to miss work and possibly cause her to make arrangements for childcare for her existing children-thus making her abortion more difficult to obtain. Time is of the essence when seeking an abortion. A day or two delay can cause a first trimester abortion to become a second trimester abortion-which is costlier and more risky.

INTAKE PROCEDURE

When you arrive at the abortion facility, you will be asked to fill out a short application. This form usually asks questions about your medical history and contact information in case of an emergency.

Before you can get an abortion, it has to be determined that you are indeed pregnant and how far along in your pregnancy that you are.

You will be given a pregnancy test and will undergo an ultrasound which will be used to accurately date your pregnancy. Your blood type will also be tested and your RH type will be noted.

PRE-ABORTION COUNSELING

The majority of abortion clinics offer some type of counseling before they perform your procedure. Depending on the facility, you may be offered one on one counseling or the counseling may take place in a group setting.

The one-on-one counseling will take place in a private area with you and an employee from the abortion clinic. The actual set up of the counseling session varies. Most of the time you will be asked if you desire an abortion and if anyone is pressuring you to have the procedure. They really try to determine that you are not being coerced or forced into getting an abortion. Next they will explain the procedure to you.

Whether you are having a first trimester abortion or a second trimester abortion, they will explain the procedure and ask you if you have any questions. This counseling session is not intended to try to talk you out of getting the procedure or to dig deep into your personal business. The main focus is to make sure that you are getting the abortion of your own free will and that you are fully aware of the procedure.

If you are not getting your procedure done at this time due to the fact of a mandatory waiting period, the counselor will give you pre- and post-abortion instructions. This may include information about whether or not you can eat before the procedure, and any other special instructions. Most clinics require that women have an escort accompany them to the clinic to drive them home after the procedure. However, if you are having a first trimester abortion, you may be able to get around this if you agree to stay in the recovery area a little bit longer after your procedure.

At this time, they may also ask you if you have any birth control plans in place for the future. Depending on the clinic, they may give you birth control, such as a Depo Provera shot or a pack of birth control pills. Other clinics may refer you to your regular Ob/Gyn or arrange birth control methods when you return for you follow up visit.

The group counseling is similar to the one on one counseling, except that it takes place within a group setting. You will be placed in a group with other women who are planning to have abortions. If the facility offers both first trimester and second trimester abortions, they may separate the counseling sessions and have women attend the session that applies to their length in their pregnancy.

In the group counseling session, the counselor will not put any one woman on the spot and ask her specific questions about her situation-in most cases. In the group counseling session, the counselor will explain the procedure and pre- and post-abortion procedures. At this time, they may ask the group which women are interested in obtaining birth control that day.

If the facility has a mandatory waiting period, the women will return the following day to have the procedure performed. If there is not a waiting period, the women usually will proceed to have the procedure performed after the counseling session.

In many instances, the facility will offer one on one counseling for the second trimester procedure. This is due to the fact that second trimester abortions are not as common as first trimester abortions and the woman has been pregnant longer and may need in depth counseling before actually having the procedure.

THE EARLY OPTION MEDICINAL ABORTION

The abortion pill or Mifeprex was approved by the FDA for abortions up to 7 weeks of gestation in the year 2000. The introduction of this drug into American society gave women an alternative to a surgical abortion. Mifeprex allows an abortion to occur by blocking the hormones necessary to allow a pregnancy to continue. Mifeprex is used in combination with Misoprostol. Misoprostol is a prostaglandin that causes the uterus to contract. The drugs must be administered by a physician.

After you take the first dose of the drugs you will experience cramping and bleeding. The pregnancy will be terminated in 24 hours in most cases. A woman who decides on a medicinal abortion will usually have to visit her health care provider three times.

When Mifeprex is used in conjunction with Misoprostol the results are 90% effective. If for some reason the medicinal abortion fails, which occurs in less than 10% of procedures, the woman will have to follow up with a surgical abortion.

Bleeding and cramping are a normal part of the procedure. Some side effects include headaches, nausea, vomiting, diarrhea, dizziness, and fatigue. Not all women will experience these side effects. If any of the side effects become severe you should contact the doctors office where you had the procedure performed immediately.

Medicinal abortions have been performed in Europe for years and the procedure is popular. The procedure is gaining in popularity in the United States as more abortion facilities begin to offer medicinal abortions.

THE ABORTION PROCEDURE –FIRST TRIMESTER

The first trimester abortion procedure is far less evasive and lengthy as the second trimester abortion procedure. You will be wearing a hospital gown and be required to lay down and place your feet in stirrups. The doctor performing the procedure and a nurse will be in attendance. Prior to the procedure you may be given the option to choose the type of anesthesia that you would prefer. Some clinics offer general (asleep) anesthesia for first trimester abortions. This type of anesthesia may cost more. Other anesthesia types are twilight (conscious) or local (numb the area, awake). Patients receiving anesthesia will be closely monitored with special attention given to blood pressure and vital signs. A gynecologist with special expertise in abortions performs the procedure by a method known as vacuum aspiration. If you are 10 weeks or less, and if available, you may be given your abortion by manual aspiration. This involves the use of a specially designed syringe to apply suction.

If manual aspiration is not available or if you are 12 weeks or less, your abortion may be performed by a vacuum machine. This is the most common first trimester abortion procedure. This method involves the use of a hollow tube that is attached by tubing to a bottle and a pump, which provides a gentle vacuum. The tube, which is called a Cannula is passed into the uterus, the pump is turned on, and the tissue is gently removed from the uterus. If all of the tissues are not removed you may be given a D&C. D&C is short for dilation and cutterage and it involves removing any remaining tissues after the aspiration procedure.

The procedure lasts anywhere from 7-15 minutes. After the procedure, the tissues removed will be examined to make sure that the abortion was complete. Some clinics take it a step further and also provide a post-abortion ultrasound.

First-trimester therapeutic surgical abortions are safe and effective and have few complications. About 90% of all abortions are done in the first trimester of pregnancy.

THE SECOND TRIMESTER ABORTION

The second trimester abortion is a two step procedure in most cases, but increasingly many clinics are offering safe second trimester abortions in a one step setting. However, the majority of abortion clinics still perform second trimester abortions in two steps.

Due to the fact that the pregnancy has progressed, you will have to be dilated before the procedure can be performed. Small sticks known as laminara or some other type of synthetic dilator will be inserted into the cervix to help open the cervix. Opening the cervix protects the cervix during the procedure and allows the instruments to not harm the cervix during the procedure. Once the artificial dilators are inserted, the woman will leave the facility and return in 18-24 hours to have the procedure performed.

Similar to the first trimester abortion, you will be wearing a hospital type gown and be required to lie on a table with your feet in stirrups. Your vital signs will be monitored and you will be given anesthesia. Depending on how many weeks you are and your preference, you may be given a general (asleep) anesthesia versus an awake form of anesthesia. If you are given general anesthesia you will only be given enough to last during the time needed to complete the procedure and you will wake up shortly after the procedure.

The second trimester abortion involves getting a D&E. D&E is short for a procedure known as dilation and evacuation. This procedure is similar to a D&C, but it involves several methods. A D&E can consist of a combination of vacuum aspiration, D&C, and the use of surgical instruments such as forceps. The D&E procedure usually lasts 30 minutes.

After the procedure, tissues are examined and an ultrasound may also be performed to ensure that the abortion process was complete.

RECOVERY

The recovery period after an abortion is very important. The abortion facility will have to monitor you and your bleeding after the procedure. The main things that they will be monitoring you for are heavy bleeding and fevers. Heavy bleeding can indicate a serious condition and a fever can be a sign of infection. You will be asked to lie down and they will give you a light snack and something to drink. This usually consists of graham crackers or saltines and juice. You will be given post-operative medications and any antibiotics you will need to take.

For first trimester abortions they may require you to stay in the recovery area for 45 minutes to an hour. For second trimester abortions you will most likely have to remain at the facility for several hours after your procedure.

Before leaving the clinic, they will once again explain after-care procedures. They may schedule a follow-up appointment at that facility or you may schedule a follow-up visit with your regular doctor at a later date. They will also provide you with any birth control that you may have requested.

HOW YOU WILL FEEL AFTERWARDS

Women report different feelings after an abortion. Some women experience only light cramps similar to menstrual cramps. Others report severe cramping. Where some women bleed only for a few days after the procedure, others may bleed for several weeks after the procedure. No one can predict and tell you how you will feel emotionally and physically after the procedure. The range of emotions experienced varies from woman to woman. If you feel severely depressed or even that you just need to talk to someone, there are many places out there that can offer you the post abortion counseling that you need.

AFTER-CARE

After your abortion you will be released from the clinic. The clinic may provide you with antibiotics. It is important that you take all of the medication given to you. You will also be provided with after care instructions. It is important to follow these directions very carefully. Failure to follow the instructions may lead to an infection or another pregnancy. Common after care instructions include:

No bathing
No douching
No insertion of any medications or tampons in the vagina
No sexual intercourse for 1-2 weeks

THE FOLLOW-UP VISIT

2-3 weeks after your abortion you will be attending a follow up visit with your regular physician or at the facility that performed your abortion. At this time a pelvic exam will be administered and you will also be given a pregnancy test. The reason that a pregnancy test is administered is to guarantee a negative result.

The doctor may ask you how your current method of birth control is working and may permit you to have sex again. Depending on the procedure you had, you may have been required to wait one or two weeks before resuming sexual intercourse.

An induced abortion rarely affects your future fertility. Most women who have abortions go on to have children if they so desire. It is important to use a reliable method of birth control following your procedure because you will be able to conceive soon after.

Some abortion facilities offer counseling at the follow up visit.

STORIES OF ABORTIONS

Shelia - Age 27
My Theory

"We all end up here again in six months. That is the first thing that I want to say. At the clinic, when you get the counseling and talk with the other girls, everyone explains how they got pregnant. Then everyone talks all this jazz about how they are never going to have sex again, or always use protection. Then in the heat of the moment, we get all hot and our bodies feel warm and we think to ourselves, "Maybe just this one time without a condom," or "I forgot to take my pill today, but just this one time nothing will happen." That kind of behavior and we end up right back here. I guess you would call us "repeat offenders." I have been to this clinic four times and recognize faces at this point. I don't use abortion as a form of birth control, I just make poor decisions. I'm no different than the others. As I say these words today, I say I'm going to do better, but at the same time, I can't say you'll never see me up in here again."

Amber - Age 22
Mr. Right Turned Out To Be Mr. Wrong

"I had been dating Eric for 3 years when I got pregnant. I was a senior in college and he had just graduated. I was living in Virginia and he was attending law school in North Carolina. We really only had time to see each other on alternating weekends. We had been sexually active for our entire relationship. With him away most of the time, I stopped using the pill. We never used condoms because we were in a monogamous relationship. One particular weekend we had sex and I told him to "pull out," but he didn't. I didn't think I could get pregnant that one time but I did.

"Initially, I considered keeping the baby. I was almost finished with college and Eric was in law school. The timing was poor, but we had talked of marriage in the past. I thought we would just change our plans and get married sooner. When I told Eric I was pregnant he totally flipped. He told me we were 'too young,' and that he had 'just started law school,' and that I was 'trying to trap him and tie him down.' I couldn't believe he said those things to me. I was devastated and thought about having the baby on my own. But then I talked to my parents and friends and decided that not having the baby would be best. There were so many things I wanted to do in life, and having a baby at that moment, and doing it on my own, would have changed everything in my life.

"We agreed on me having an abortion and Eric was a jerk about it. He didn't even come to take me to get the procedure. He paid for it, but get this—he had one of his frat brothers drop the money off at my door one evening.

"After the abortion I was depressed. It didn't hurt too bad and the procedure went rather quickly. I was sad because a part of me wanted to keep the baby. I was also sad because I couldn't believe how fast Eric changed on me. After the abortion Eric and I never talked again. Now I am 26 years old and happily married to a wonderful man with a baby on the way. All I can say is everything happens for a reason."

Vita - Age 28
Ultimately It Was My Decision

"I am married with three children. My husband and I both are in the Navy. It is very hard to be married and have three children, not to mention we both are on ships that go out to sea for deployments of up to six months or more at a time.

"Thanksgiving we took a trip to Mississippi to visit family. I was sick and throwing up the whole trip. I knew I was pregnant. Our youngest child was only 15 months old, and I couldn't imagine having another child that soon. Truthfully, I didn't want any more children, but my husband wanted more and I knew he would be excited about the pregnancy. He was pro-life and strongly against abortion.

"As soon as we got home to Virginia, I took a pregnancy test and it was positive. I immediately took the positive test outside to the trash dumpster so my husband wouldn't find it. I called the clinic to schedule an abortion. By my calculations I was only 4-5 weeks pregnant and they said they wouldn't schedule me until I was at least 7 ½-8 weeks pregnant. So for almost 3 weeks I had to hide my pregnancy from my husband. I told him that I had a stomach virus and he was none the wiser. I had my girlfriend take me to get the abortion, and afterwards I went home and pretended to feel fine even though I was tired and cramping. I told my husband I was just having a heavy period.

"This was the second abortion that I had. I feel that as a grown woman I should be able to make decisions about my body without the government or even my husband stepping in. Some people might say I was wrong, but ultimately it was my decision."

Caitlin - Age 16
A Really Bad Experience

"I was raised in Albany, New York. My home life was stable. I had two parents who adored me and a wonderful little brother. When I started high school, I don't know if I was rebelling or what, but my best friend Rachel and I really got into the whole 'goth' thing. I dyed my blonde hair jet black, and I pierced my tongue, lip and eye brow. I only wore black and my parents hated it. They always told me I needed counseling, but at the same time, my grades didn't drop so they couldn't complain too much. They chalked it up as me going through a phase.

"One day sophomore year, Rachel and I cut class and decided to hang out at my friend Frankie's house. He was goth too. We listened to music and had a couple of drinks. There was a guy over there named Chad. He was 24, goth, and he was cute. Rachel and I had never seen him before, but since he was Frankie's friend he was cool. We all did some 'E' that day, but it was no big deal because we had done 'E' before.

"Rachel and Frankie left to go to the grocery store to get something or other. I was out of it from the alcohol and the 'E' but I was well aware of what was going on. Chad asked me to come in Frankie's bedroom and listen to a CD that they had made. I didn't think anything of it so I followed him into the bedroom. Once we got in there he held me down on the bed and started to pull down my pants. I begged him to stop and he grabbed my breast and stuck his tongue in my mouth. He raped me for what seemed like hours, but was in all actuality only about 20 minutes. I didn't scream because no one was in the house. When he heard Rachel and Frankie return from the store he stopped.

"I didn't report the rape to the authorities because I had been drinking and using drugs and I thought no one would believe me. About a month later, I discovered I was pregnant. I was 15 years old, and I was in no way ready to become a parent. I confided in my mother that I was pregnant and we made arrangements for me to have an abortion. I kept the rape a secret, and I did not reveal to her who the father of the child was.

"I didn't have an abortion just because I conceived during a rape. I was young and wasn't ready to be a parent. I do not feel guilty about having the abortion and I don't believe I bear any emotional scars from the abortion. However, I feel that I am still recovering from the emotional trauma of the rape."

Cynthia - Age 15
A game with real life consequences

"One month I had a period and the next month I didn't. I was 12 years old and I didn't think anything of it. When I told my mom that my period had stopped coming, she never imagined that I might be pregnant. She called our family doctor who advised her that sometimes young women have irregular menstrual cycles.

"I guess I should start at the beginning. My name is Cynthia and when I was 12 years old I got pregnant. I didn't know I had sex. I thought I was still a virgin. So how did I end up pregnant?

"At my cousin Sheri's 14th Halloween party, we played a game of 'truth or dare.' We were too old for costumes and we were just having a good time playing games and eating candy and pizza. I had on a short skirt and a tight shirt. I was the youngest at the party. My breasts were just starting to grow in. Some of the kids at the party dared me to go into the closet with a boy named Vincent and to let him stick his thing in me for one minute.

"I didn't want to seem like a party pooper and I wanted to be like the older girls who had been doing wild dares all night. I followed Vincent, who was 14 into the closet. Everyone wanted to watch! They said they wanted to make sure we did it. I said, 'Can you please close the door?' They closed the closet door and everyone started to mock me, 'Can you please close the door.'

"In the closet I lifted up my skirt and kept my panties on. Vincent pulled down his pants and tried to put his thing in me. I don't even know if he got it in all the way. Before I knew it, my panties were all wet and the group outside opened the door and started pointing and laughing. That Monday, everyone at school teased me for going in the closet with Vincent.

My period stopped coming and I didn't think anything about it. I didn't know I was pregnant. My breasts grew bigger and my hips got bigger. I was in 7th grade and more boys started to like me. My mom and I chalked it up to puberty, until one day my mother and I were at Sears trying on clothes and she looked at my stomach. She asked me if I was pregnant and I said 'No.'

"Soon after my mother took me to the doctor and discovered I was pregnant. I wasn't just a little pregnant. I was real pregnant. I was about 17 ½ weeks. My mother pressured me about who I was having sex with, and I hadn't had sex with anyone. I thought she meant recently, at least in the last few months. I didn't know anything about being pregnant. It didn't take long for me to tell my mother about the Halloween party.

"I didn't have a choice, my mother was taking me to get an

abortion. I didn't know what I wanted, but then again I was a baby myself.

"The first clinic we went to didn't take patients under 13 years of age, due to the fact that their bodies are still developing and so on. Then all of the other clinics in our area only offered first trimester abortions.

"My mother ended up taking me to another state to get an abortion. I remember us being turned away by so many clinics due to my age. When we finally found a clinic, it was costly, $1400. That was a lot of money and I knew my mom didn't have any money to spare. She took a cash advance off of her credit card to pay for the procedure.

"At the clinic I was counseled, and when I found out what an abortion was, I changed my mind. I didn't want to have one. I wanted to keep the baby. My mother was not hearing me though, and since she was my guardian, she pretty much ran the situation.

"After the abortion, I remember waking up after the procedure and thrashing my body all about and I fell off of the recovery room table. I was screaming and crying. I was having horrible cramps and I felt bad because the baby I just found out about a few days earlier was gone. I cried the whole time in the recovery room and the whole ride home. I was bleeding so much, and so depressed that my mom let me stay home a whole week from school.

"It was a bad situation, but now that I am older I realize that my mom did the right thing for me at the time. I'm a freshman in high school, and very active in school. I still consider myself a virgin because that incident was so strange. I love my mom and I'm glad that she did what she did for me. I couldn't imagine being someone's parent right now. Everything worked out for me thanks to her persistence and love for me."

CHAPTER 4 - Adoption - Giving Your Child A Loving Chance

WHAT IS ADOPTION?

Adoption is the act of giving your child to another family to raise. Adoption is a legal act, and by choosing adoption you will permanently give your child to another family to raise. If you choose adoption, there are many people and organizations that can help you proceed with your decision.

Adoption does not have to be a scary thing. It can be a loving choice for you and your child. You can choose to have an open adoption or a private adoption.

OPEN ADOPTION

An open adoption is one where the birth parents and the adoptive parents have knowledge of one another. Often, the birth mother will interview prospective adoptive parents. If the two agree on an open adoption, they may decide on a level of contact to continue after the birth of the child. Sometimes the birth mother and the adoptive parents will agree that the adoptive parents send pictures. Some open adoptions go as far as to allow the birth mother to have visitation rights. The level of openness is dependent on the parties involved. Any type of open adoption agreement should be legally binding and a lawyer should be involved.

CONFIDENTIAL ADOPTION

In a confidential adoption, the birth parents and the adoptive parents do not know each others identity. The only information that the prospective adoptive parents are given about you and the birth father is your medical history.

PRIVATE ADOPTION

A private adoption is one that does not go through an adoption agency.

A private adoption is one where the birth mother has no contact with the birth parents after the adoption. The birth mother can view profiles of prospective birth parents and choose a family for her child. The birth parents and the prospective adoptive parents work through a licensee. The birth parents will have to sign a consent form to release the child to the adoptive family. Although a consent form is signed, the birth parents will have a window in time in which they can change their mind and get their child back. The time allowed for reversing a private adoption varies from state to state.

Sometimes there are degrees of contact with a private adoption. Often the birth parents and the adoptive parents will set up an agreement with a lawyer, third party to send non identifying pictures to the birth parents.

Depending on your adoption situation, the prospective parents or the adoption agency may pay for your prenatal care and delivery if you do not have insurance.

Research any agency that you plan to deal with carefully. If they ever ask you for money, look elsewhere. The birth mother should not have to pay a listing fee or any type of fees when they choose to place their child up for adoption.

CONSENT

Whether you are married or single, to place your child up for adoption, you and the birth father will have to sign a document terminating parental rights. A biological father, or alleged biological father, has to consent to adoption if he has been notified that he is the father and has taken steps to support the child.

A putative father is the alleged father of a child born out of wedlock. A putative father has no legal rights to a child until he has taken action to establish paternity. He must establish paternity to receive notice of adoption proceedings or to contest an adoption.

Different states have different laws regarding putative fathers rights with regards to adoption. When you begin the adoption process you will be informed of the steps you need to take in regards to the child's father and the adoption process.

GETTING STARTED WITH THE ADOPTION PROCESS

If you have chosen or are leaning in the direction of adoption it is important to start planning your child's adoption early in your pregnancy. Part of the planning includes educating yourself on the adoption process and the adoption laws in your state. The resources below can assist you in getting started with the adoption process.

National Adoption Information Clearinghouse

The National Adoption Information Clearinghouse is a resource with a wealth of information on adoption. The Clearinghouse is a service of Children's Bureau, Administration on Children, Youth and Families, Administration for Children and Families, Department of Health and Human Services. Their services for birth mothers are free. This should be your first step when considering adoption versus just jumping on the Internet. They are not an adoption agency but they can provide you with educational materials about adoption. They can also give you listings for adoption agencies and Crisis Pregnancy Centers in your area that can assist with your adoption. Their web site URL can be found in the web resources section of this book.

Crisis Pregnancy Centers

Crisis Pregnancy Centers provide free, confidential services to pregnant women. They not only provide free pregnancy testing and counseling, but they also provide adoption support and assistance. Many Crisis Pregnancy Centers also are licensed adoption agencies.

Adoption Agencies

An adoption agency is a licensed agency that provides services to birth parents and adoptive parents. Adoption agencies can be non-profit, for profit, religious based, public or private. When choosing an agency, make sure that the agency is licensed. If they ask you for any money, this can be a red flag. The birth mother should not have to pay any money, such as for a listing fee, when she is considering adoption.

Health Department or Social Services

If you contact your local health department they can refer you to the appropriate state agency that can assist you with your adoption.

PROTECT YOURSELF

It is important that you have an attorney or an advocate that is knowledgeable about the adoption process that will represent you and make sure that your wishes are being followed and that the best interest of you and your child are primary. Even if your resources are low, you may be able to find an adoption attorney.

FUTURE CONTACT

You may decide that you want to find your child one day when they become an adult or, vice versa, your child may decide to seek you one day. If you choose a confidential adoption, there may be ways for you to leave information about yourself to help your child locate you in the future. Many states have set up adoption registries. The way that the registries work is that you submit information about yourself and the birth of the child to the registry. You will leave your phone number and address with the registry. If the child decides to search for you in the future and the information that they have regarding their birth matches up with the information provided by you, the registry will release your information to the child.

Another method is that some adoption agencies and lawyers who handle adoptions will keep a letter in the child's file that has specific information about you and how to contact you. Not all attorneys and agencies will agree to this in a confidential adoption, so you may wish to choose an agency that will follow your wishes. Remember, this is your child and you have rights on how you want your adoption to be carried through.

STORIES OF ADOPTION

Heather - Age 18
A Very Different Story of Adoption

"My story of adoption is one of love and very different than any other one that you may have heard before. I was raised by my mother in a loving single parent home. I never met my dad, but my mother loved me enough for two parents. I was a popular high school student. I was athletic and played softball and volleyball. I started dating Chad, a football player during my sophomore year. We were really a close couple and I lost my virginity to him. At 17, I became pregnant. My mother and I are very close, so I immediately told her. She was supportive and told me that she was 100% behind me no matter what my decision. I never considered abortion, although Chad did initially. My mother was 18 when I was born, and if she would have aborted me, I wouldn't be here today. We narrowed down our decision to keeping the baby or giving it up for adoption.

"When I was 3 months pregnant, the obstetrician discovered that I was pregnant with twins. This information not only shocked me, it overwhelmed me. I could imagine myself taking care of one baby and finishing school, but the thought of taking care of two babies was overwhelming.

"I contacted several adoption agencies and was flooded with information from prospective birth parents. I am a white female with blonde hair and blue eyes and when they discovered that the birth father was a white male, things really heated up. I realized that my twins were a hot commodity. I even had some prospective birth parents contact me outside of the agency offering me up to $50,000 for one or both of my babies.

"I have a loving Christian church family and they were supportive. I never considered 'selling' my baby to the highest bidder. I was leaning toward adoption when the Johnsons came into my life. They were a loving couple who attended my church. Mrs. Johnson was a school teacher and unable to have children on her own. They couldn't have children of their own and had adopted a little girl two years earlier.

"After many conversations with God, the Johnsons, my mother and with Chad, we decided to place one of the babies with the Johnsons and I would raise the other one. People feel very strongly against splitting up twins, and initially Chad was against it. However, we discussed an open adoption. Which meant I would have some visitation, we would exchange pictures and so on. The Johnsons attended my church, and Mrs. Johnson assured me that she would make sure that the boys knew of each other growing up. No matter what the situation, I advise anyone planning an adoption to get a lawyer involved to protect your rights.

"It was very hard for me to choose which baby I would place for adoption and which one I would keep. I won't reveal how I made my final decision. It was so hard looking into those precious faces and having to choose to give one away. I cried for weeks, but I felt an enormous sense of love and warmth that I was helping another couple. I also agonized that the baby I gave up would grow up and hate me for not keeping him.

"Three years later, I am a college student and the mother of two boys. Chad is active in my son's life although he and I are not a couple anymore. Although, I gave one of my sons to Mrs. Johnson, she is his mother, but I also feel like I am his mother. The Johnsons kept their word about an open adoption and they invite me and my son Danny over for play dates every month.

"It was a hard decision, but I did what I did for love."

Sue - Age 28
The Child My Family Will Never Know

"I came to the United States on a student visa to study medicine. I came to the US from Japan. I am the youngest child of my parents and I have three older brothers. It was difficult for me to convince my parents to send me to the US to continue my education. They felt like there were plenty of good schools in Japan and being the only female, they weren't quite sure I needed to become a doctor.

"I desperately wanted to prove them wrong and succeed. During my last year of medical school I was dating another medical student named Robert. Unexpectedly, I became pregnant. Neither of us were ready to be parents. Robert promised to support me no matter what my decision would be.

"We decided that we would place the child up for adoption. Initially, when I contacted adoption agencies, they told me that they may have a hard time placing a Japanese child, but when they found out the father was white, they said that may help me find an adoptive family easier.

"Robert and I screened every family carefully and we were lucky enough to find an Asian woman and a white male who were looking for a bi-racial child. This was wonderful because I was concerned about my child being raised by 100% non Asian parents.

"It was hard for me to sign away the baby boy Robert and I had, but it was for the best. I finished my residency after medical school and only plan on staying in the United States for a few more years. I plan to return to Japan permanently to be near my family.

"My family and I are very close, yet I never told them about the child I gave birth to. I feel bad because my family is so close and it is hard to imagine that part of my family blood line is out there and will never know us."

Nancy - age 18
Foster care, a baby and a young girl without a home

"When I was 15 years old, my life was in turmoil to say the least. I never knew my father. My mother was a drug addict who died of AIDS when I was 13 years old. I was placed in the custody of my aunt who was very strict. I couldn't take it and I ran away to live on the streets. My aunt was determined not to let me slip away, so she made sure that I was placed in foster care. I soon became a ward of the state. I bounced from foster home to foster home.

"I had a boyfriend named Ted. He was much older than me, he was in his twenties. I would hide out at his house instead of going to school and we would drink and have sex.

"My foster mother suspected I was pregnant and took me to the doctor. I was 4 ½ months pregnant when I found out I was pregnant. It wasn't too late to have an abortion, but I actually considered keeping the baby. When I told Ted, he told me that I was a 'runaway, throw-away slut' and that the baby probably wasn't his. I still wanted to keep the baby.

"My foster mother was in 'too deep,' she said. She turned me back over to the court system. They placed me in a home for girls. Since I was a ward of the state, they told me that I would either have to stay in the girls home or find a foster parent that was willing to take me and my baby. My baby was going to born a ward of the state! I couldn't have that. I didn't have anything. I felt like the best thing would be to place the child up for adoption.

"I learned a little bit about the adoptive parents, their careers and about their other kids and decided to go the adoption route. I gave birth to a healthy baby girl at 8 months and she was adopted shortly after.

"Three years later, a part of me really regrets my decision. Now I am 18, I finished my GED and I have my own apartment. I work and I am planning to go to city college. I wish that more people would have taken an interest in me and helped me see that I could have kept my baby and been all right. But I hope that she has a nice life now."

Diane - age 22
I never wanted to even look at the baby

"My boyfriend and I were together for 3 years before we had our first child. Our son Abe meant the world to us. After Abe was born, my boyfriend started drinking more and we argued more than ever. When our son was two years old I found out that I was pregnant again. We immediately knew that we were not ready for more kids. We were having a hard enough time being college students having one child. I had planned on having an abortion but time slipped away and I didn't have the money for the more costly second trimester procedure. So we decided to give the baby up for adoption.

"I did not become attached to this baby. I tried to ignore the babies kicks and I didn't even want to look at the ultrasound picture. When my boyfriend found out the baby was another boy he started having second thoughts.

"My mind was made up. When I went into labor, I didn't even pack a bag for the new baby. When I gave birth, I told the doctor I didn't even want to see the baby. After the baby was born they took him straight to the nursery. Before I was discharged I signed the adoption papers.

"I never did see the baby. My boyfriend went down to the nursery and held the baby and cried. He told me the baby had my blue eyes.

"It may sound cold hearted that I never saw the baby, but I knew I would just melt. I had to stay strong to follow through with my decision.

"The whole adoption thing really caused us a lot of emotional distress. My boyfriend would always remind me of the baby we had given away and I never wanted to talk about it. Our two year old Abe also suffered because we were such an emotional wreck we weren't there for him.

"We eventually decided to go into counseling and gradually things are coming around."

CHAPTER 5:
Abandonment and Infanticide - Never Options but Information You Should Know

Child abandonment should never be considered a viable option when faced with an unplanned pregnancy. Child abandonment of newborns has only slightly risen over the past decade, but cases are receiving more media attention than they have in the past. Desperation has driven young mothers to dispose of their newborn infants in toilets and garbage cans. Many of these mothers managed to conceal their pregnancy and were full term at the time they delivered.

Leslie Harris shocked the film industry in 1993 with the release of her independent film, *Just Another Girl on The IRT*. The film won a special Jury Prize at the 1993 Sundance Film Festival and was distributed by Miramax.

The film tells the story of a teenage girl named Chantel Mitchell who had high hopes and aspirations for the future. Raised in the projects of New York by poor working class parents, Chantel had her sites set on graduating from high school a year early and heading to college.

Chantel's plans were sidetracked when she finds herself pregnant. Chantel acts in a behavior that is typical of many young women facing an unplanned pregnancy. She is scared, and she tries to push her pregnancy to the back of her mind. Chantel hides her pregnancy, only revealing it to her boyfriend and a clinic worker. Her boyfriend pressures her to have an abortion and he even goes as far to give Chantel the money for the procedure. Chantel uses the money to go on a shopping spree with her friend. Chantel never followed through with the abortion.

With no prenatal care, Chantel goes into premature labor at 29 weeks. With her boyfriends assistance, they wrap the baby in a plastic bag and dispose of the baby outside in a trash dumpster. However, second thoughts prevent them from actually following through.

Sadly, many women feel so desperate that they simply feel the urge to "get rid of the baby." Sometimes they feel so desperate that they don't care about the safety or the well being of the infant, as long as the child is gone they feel as if their problem will be solved.

Abandonment or infanticide should never be considered an option when there are so many safe options for women facing unwanted pregnancy. Infanticide is the murder of an infant born alive. The Amy Grossburg and Brian Peterson Case gained national attention in 1996 when the two high school sweethearts were suspected of killing their newborn son and leaving the infant in a motel trash dumpster. Grossburg had managed to conceal her pregnancy from her family and gave birth to a healthy full term boy. The couple later pled guilty to manslaughter charges and served less than three years in prison.

Another infanticide case that drew national attention was the case of New Jersey V. Melissa Drexler, a case often referred to as "The Prom Mom" case. Eighteen year old Melissa Drexler concealed her pregnancy from her family, friends, and even the suspected child's father-her 19 year old prom date. On the morning of her prom, the 130 pound teen's water broke. Soon after arriving at the prom, Melissa experienced cramping and went into the bathroom where she delivered a full term baby boy. After strangling the infant and placing him in numerous garbage bags, Melissa threw the infant in a garbage can and returned to the prom.

Melissa initially was to face murder charges, but after pleading guilty to a lesser charge she read the following statement in court:

"I knew I was pregnant. I concealed the pregnancy from everyone. On the morning of the prom my water broke. While I was in the car on the way to the prom, I began to have cramps. I went to the prom and I went into the bathroom and delivered the baby. The baby was born alive. I knowingly took the baby out the toilet and wrapped a series of garbage bags around the baby. I then placed the baby in another garbage bag, knotted it closed and threw it in the trash can. I was aware of what I was doing at the time when I placed the baby in the bag. And I was further aware that what I did would most certainly result in the death of the baby."

In 1998, Melissa Drexler was sentenced to 15 years in prison. She was released in 2001 after serving nearly 4 years in prison. The infanticide cases mentioned are tragic and the worst possible result of infant abandonment. Several states have enacted a very controversial law that allows mothers the opportunity to leave their newborn infants at so called "safe havens" with no questions asked and facing no criminal charges, as long as the infants are healthy. Although the actual type of "safe haven" varies from state to state, most of the states that support this legislation allow the mothers to leave the newborns at police stations, fire stations, and hospitals. The laws also vary from state to state. Texas was the first state to sign the "Baby Moses" legislation under then Governor George W. Bush.

Many argue that Safe Haven legislation is telling the mother that it is okay to just abandon her child. However, with child abandonment and infanticide taking place anyway, Safe Haven legislation offers a safe alternative for the extremely desperate birth mother.

After the infants are left at Safe Havens, they are first given physical examinations to determine whether they are in good health. Then depending on the state, most of the children are either placed in foster care or immediately placed for adoption.

A STORY OF ABANDONMENT

BARBARA - age 39
(As told by her neighbor Stephanie)

"Barbara became pregnant for the first time at the age of 39. She lived next door to me in an apartment complex. We became good friends during the time we were neighbors. An unmarried secretary, who lived a modest lifestyle, Barbara was initially happy about her pregnancy. The child's father was a truck driver that she had been dating on and off for three years.

"As Barbara's pregnancy progressed, her boyfriend began to call less and less. She became depressed and began to resent the fact that she was carrying his child. She eventually began to regret the entire pregnancy.

"Barbara had no immediate family in the area where we lived. I helped her as much as I could. After giving birth, she depended on me more and more to help her care for the child. By this point, the boyfriend had completely stopped coming around and called on the phone less and less.

"Barbara who lived in Dallas, was determined to see her boyfriend. When the child was 3 weeks old, she drove to Indiana with the child to see the boyfriend.

"The trip obviously did not go well, because when she returned to Dallas she was more and more despondent and depressed. As the weeks went by, I noticed her slowly moving her belongings out of her apartment. When I asked her if she was moving she said, 'No.'

"One rainy Thursday evening, Barbara knocked on my door and begged me to keep her baby, whom she had named Grace. I recall that Barbara seemed desperate and confused. It was after 11PM and I was sleeping, but Barbara begged, claiming that she had to, 'Go to the bus station to pick up her mother who was visiting from Louisiana.' When I heard the words 'bus station,' and taking into consideration Barbara's strange behavior, I got an eerie feeling that Barbara was not planning to come back. I told her 'I can't keep Grace,' and Barbara dropped the infant carrier and the screaming infant in my doorway and ran into the night.

"Several days passed and Barbara never called or came by to pick up Grace. I called the landlord and asked him if he had heard from Barbara. He informed me that Barbara had moved out and picked up her deposit. It was a hard thing to do but I called social services and turned over the child to the state protective agency.

"Three weeks later there was a knock at my door. It was Barbara. I was not extremely shocked because I always had a gut feeling that she would make contact again with me one way or another. I invited Barbara in. She refused, and only stood in the doorway.

"'Girl, I am so sorry. I ended up taking the bus to Indiana to see Ronald, I was planning to come right back. Where's Gracie?' she asked. I explained that I had turned the child over to social services. Barbara seemed a bit saddened and I explained that if she explained her situation to the social worker who was handling Grace's case, perhaps they could help her regain custody of the child.

" I handed Barbara the social workers card and she left. Barbara never called the social worker and I later learned that Barbara was still living in the Dallas area. Grace was eventually adopted by a family.

"It's a sad thing, I can't imagine someone leaving their baby like that, but I suppose she was in a desperate situation."

CHAPTER 6:
After Your Pregnancy - Birth Control for the Future

CONTRACEPTION

After your pregnancy has ended, whether you continued your pregnancy to term or you terminated your pregnancy, you may initially think that you won't have sex again for a very long time. Your body will heal and you will most likely engage in sexual activity again in your lifetime.

Rather than just swearing that you will never have sex again, (although it is your right to pursue abstinence), it's better to plan ahead for your next sexual encounter. If you are prepared, you can take the necessary steps to prevent another unplanned pregnancy. More than 3 million unintended pregnancies occur every year in the United States. The 3 million women who use no contraceptives account for almost half of these pregnancies (47%), while the 39 million method users account for 53%.

Abstinence
Abstinence is the act of refraining from sexual intercourse. Abstinence is the safest method of birth control. Refraining from sexual intercourse will definitely eliminate any chance of becoming pregnant. However, some people may find abstinence a difficult method of birth control and others may not consider it at all. If you do consider abstinence or another form of abstinence called "Second

Virginity" there are many support groups that will help you with your decision.

The Birth Control Pill

The birth control pill is the most popular reversible birth control method on the market. Birth control pills are oral hormones that when taken daily prevent pregnancy. The pills come in packs of 21 or 28 pills. When used daily without user error, the Pill is 95% effective. The Pill does have some added benefits such as reduced menstrual bleeding and cramps and a reduction to the risk of ovarian cancer. The pill is available from a doctor via prescription. Women who smoke or have heart conditions should not consider taking the Pill. These women face an increased risk of heart attacks and blood clots. The pill has been around since the 1960's and is a highly effective choice for birth control. The pill is reversible and women can conceive after cessation of pill use.

Common Complaints:

Some have trouble remembering to take the Pill daily

Some women claim the Pill causes weight gain, headaches and moodiness

Depo-Provera

Depo-Provera is commonly known as "The Birth Control Shot." Depo-Provera is a form of birth control administered via a shot that will prevent pregnancy for three months at a time. If Depo-Provera is a woman's choice for birth control, she will only have to worry about birth control 4 times a year. Depo-Provera prevents pregnancy by releasing a hormone similar to progesterone. The popularity of Depo-Provera grew in the 1990's. Depo-Provera can be administered by a doctor, nurse or health care professional. Depo-Provera is reversible and it is 99% effective when preventing pregnancy.

Common Complaints:
  Weight gain
  Irregularity or cessation of menstrual cycles

Male Condoms

Condoms are a popular form of contraceptive. A woman doesn't have to alter her body with hormones. Male condoms place the responsibility of birth control on the male sex partner. Condoms are a barrier method of birth control, which means they prevent sperm from entering the vaginal canal. They are 86% effective and inexpensive, costing about .25 cents to .50 cents each. To increase the effectiveness of condoms, they should be used in conjunction with spermicide.

Common Complaints:
Can tear or slip off
Effectiveness based on using the condom every time sexual intercourse takes place
Some men complain of decrease in sexual pleasure

Female Condom

The female condom is available but has not gained as much popularity as the male condom. The female condom is more expensive. They average about $3 each. The female condom is worn inside of the vagina and its edges cover the woman's genitalia. Like the male condom, the female condom is available at drug stores without a prescription.

Common Complaints:
Often difficult to use and can slip during sexual activity

Inter Uterine Device (IUD)

An IUD is a small device implanted into the uterus to prevent pregnancy. The IUD is a device that will stay in the uterus until removed and must be inserted by a doctor. Insertion and removal will cost about $500. Some IUD's can be left in place for up to 10 years. The IUD prevents fertilization of the egg by producing a sterile inflammatory response that kills sperm. Some IUD's release progesterone and prevent implantation. A small string hangs out of the uterus into the vagina. A woman has to be able to feel this string in order to know that the IUD is in place. A woman should check the IUD string after every menstrual period. IUD's are 97% effective.

Due to some problems, the use of IUD's decreased in the United States during the 80's and 90's while the devices remained popular worldwide. The FDA recently approved the use of Mirena. Mirena is 99% effective and can be kept in place for up to 5 years if checked yearly by a doctor.

Common Complaints:
Expulsion of the IUD
Menstrual problems

Diaphram

The diaphragm is a barrier method of birth control. A diaphragm is a round dome shaped rubber device that fits inside of the vagina and covers the cervical opening. A woman has to be specially fitted for a diaphragm by a doctor and this device must be placed in the vagina prior to sexual activity. To increase the effectiveness of the diaphragm spermicide should be used. After a change in weight or child birth a woman should visit her doctor to get refitted for her diaphragm.

Common Complaints:
Inconvenient

The Birth Control Patch

Ortho Evra is the first birth control patch to be introduced on the market. The patch is a thin square that can be worn in one of four places on the body. Ortho Evra works by releasing small amounts of estrogen and progesterone into your system. The patch is 99% effect. Ortho Evra became available for prescription in April of 2002.

Common Complaints:
Headaches
Menstrual cramps
Relatively new on the market, some new users hesitant

Emergency Birth Control

Preven, or the "morning after pill" can be used within 72 hours of having unprotected sex. It is 98% effective. Preven is a form of emergency contraception and should not be used as a regular birth control method. Preven is the first FDA approved emergency contraception. Preven stops or delays ovulation after sexual intercourse has taken place. Preven is only available by prescription.

Common Complaints:
Drug stores often do not have the product in stock, thus reducing the effectiveness if a woman has to wait several days for the drug to arrive.
Woman has to visit or contact a doctor immediately in order to get the drug prescribed.

CHAPTER 7 - Web Resources

ABORTION

The National Abortion Federation
www.prochoice.org

The National Abortion Federations mission is to keep abortion safe and legal. Their web site features abortion facts, information on finding an abortion provider and links to relevant web sites.

Abortion Clinics On-Line
www.gynpages.com

Abortion Clinics On-Line is a directory service of abortion providers.

Planned Parenthood – Abortion
www.plannedparenthood.org/ABORTION/

A part of the Planned Parenthood web site, the abortion section includes factual information about the abortion procedure. Site also includes a Q&A section that features answers to common questions about abortion.

National Network of Abortion Funds
www.nnaf.org

The National Network of Abortion Funds provides support to local abortion funds, aids in the creation of new abortion funds and helps women who are having financial difficulties finding the funds for an abortion.

Mifeprex- Medical Abortion Pill RU486
www.earlyoptionpill.com
Official web site for the early option abortion pill. Site includes answers to commonly asked questions about Mifeprex and information about the history of the early option pill.

ADOPTION

National Adoption Information Clearinghouse
www.calib.com/naic
The National Adoption Information Clearinghouse is a resource with a wealth of information on adoption. The Clearinghouse is a service of Children's Bureau, Administration on Children, Youth and Families, Administration for Children and Families, Department of Health and Human Services.

Insight-Open Adoption Resources and Support
www.r2press.com
Brenda Romanchik explains the process of open adoption on her web site. She is also the author of several helpful adoption pamphlets that educate birth parents on the adoption process.

American Adoption Congress
www.americanadoptioncongress.org
The American Adoption Congress is composed of individuals, families and organizations committed to adoption reform. They represent people whose lives are touched by adoption. Their web site includes valuable information about the adoption process.

Adoption.Com-Where Families Come Together
www.adoption.com

Adoption.com is an on-line adoption resource site. Site includes information for the birth mother and prospective adoptive parents.

Lifetime Adoption Facillitation Center
www.lifetimeadoption.com
Lifetime Adoption provides birth parents with assistance in finding prospective adoptive families. Services are free to birth mothers.

ANTI-ABANDONMENT

AMT Children of Hope Foundation
www.amtchildrenofhope.com
The AMT Children of Hope Foundation is a not-for-profit organization that provides help to pregnant women in crisis. They were founded by Ambulance Medical Technicians of the Nassau County Police Department. They sponsor an emergency infant pick-up hotline and they also provide proper burials to infants who were victims of infanticide.

Baby Moses
www.babymoses.org
The mission of the Baby Moses project is to find safe alternatives to child abandonment. Site also provides information on individual states Safe Haven legislation.

Project Cuddle
www.projectcuddle.org
The Project Cuddle web site provides a 24 hour hotline for women considering abandoning their infants. Site also features information on how Project Cuddle can assist pregnant women who are in desperate situations.

EXPECTANT MOTHERS

Storknet- Pregnancy and Parenting On-Line Community
www.storknet.com
The Storknet site features nutrition information, a baby name database, message boards and a wealth of pregnancy related information.

Babyzone- Pregnancy, Parenting and Family Planning
www.babyzone.com
Babyzone is an on-line community for the expecting parent. Site features a wealth of pregnancy related articles, links, and resources.

Pregnancy Today- Pregnancy and Baby Related Resources for Parents By Parents
www.pregnancytoday.com
The Pregnancy Today site features a daily pregnancy calendar, diaries, personal web pages and various other pregnancy and parenting related resources.

American Baby-Your Partner In Parenting
www.americanbaby.com
The American Baby site features expert advice, a pregnancy calendar, and various other parenting and pregnancy related information. You can also subscribe to American Baby magazine for free via the web site.

Pregnancy Week By Week
www.pregnancyguideonline
Pregnancy Week by Week is a comprehensive site that features fetal developmental information about each week of pregnancy. Site also includes information about how mom to be will be feeling during her pregnancy and reviews of pregnancy books.

BREASTFEEDING

Breastfeeding.com-Information, Support and Attitude
www.breastfeeding.com

This breastfeeding web site includes a breastfeeding Q&A section, expert advice, video clips, and instructions on how to express breast milk.

La Leche League
www.lalecheleague.org

The La Leche league web site provides a wealth of breastfeeding information and a directory of local La Leche League groups.

CHILD CARE

National Child Care Information Center
www.nccic.org

The National Child Care Information Center is a national resource that ensures all children and families have access to high-quality comprehensive services.

The Original Babysitting Connection
www.babysittingconnection.com

The Original Babysitting Connection is an on-line resource that let parents search for child care providers in their area.

EMERGENCY CONTRACEPTION

Back Up Your Birth Control
www.backupyourbirthcontrol.org

This on-line campaign strives to educate women about emergency contraception.

Site includes facts and informative information about emergency contraception.

Preven
www.preven.com
Preven is the first FDA-approved product for emergency contraception.

GOVERNMENT RESOURCES

Women, Infant and Children Program (WIC)
www.fns.usda.gov/wic/
WIC is a USDA program designed to provide nutritious food supplements and education to at risk pregnant women and their children.

Food Stamp Program
www.fns.usda.gov/fsp/
The Food Stamp Program provides benefits to low income people so that they can purchase food to improve their diet.

The Administration for Children and Families
www.acf.dhhs.gov
This web site provides information on Administration for Children and Families programs including Welfare and Low Income Assistance, Child Care, Child Support, and other programs.

US Department of Health and Human Services
www.hhs.gov/agencies
The US Department of Health and Human Services web site provides links to agencies that fall under the Department of Health and Human Services, including Medicaid.

INFANT FORMULAS

Carnation Good Start
www.verybestbaby.com
The Carnation web site includes information about Carnations infant formula. Carnation also has a free magazine that expecting parents can subscribe to.

Enfamil
www.enfamil.com
The Enfamil web site features product information and child development information.

Similac
www.welcomeadditions.com
The Similac web site features product information and child development information.

MATERNITY LEAVE

Family and Medical Leave Act
http://www.dol.gov/esa/whd/fmla/
This site includes the 1993 text of the act, regulations, compliance guides, forms and related information regarding the act.

Facts About Pregnancy Discrimination
www.eeoc.gov/facts/fs-preg.html
The EEOC provides information about the Pregnancy Discrimination Act and a brief overview of a pregnant woman's rights and her employers responsibilities.

MATERNITY SHELTERS AND CRISIS SUPPORT

Lifecall
www.lifecall.org/shelters.html
The Lifecall web site features a state by state listing of maternity shelters

Children of the Night
www.childrenofthenight.org
Children of the Night is a not for profit organization dedicated to helping children between the ages of 11 and 17 who find themselves in the world of prostitution. They provide shelter and educational programs to help children in need.

Covenant House
www.covenanthouse.org
Covenant House is a private organization that provides food, shelter and clothing to homeless and runaway youths. In addition to providing shelter, they provide services in education, health care, and vocational training.

Pregnancy Center Listings
www.pregnancycenters.org
Web site features state by state listings for Crisis Pregnancy Centers

Birthright
www.birthright.org
Birthright provides guidance and assistance for women facing unplanned pregnancies. Birthright helps women find alternatives to abortion.

PARENTING SUPPORT

Girl Mom
www.girlmom.com
Girl Mom is a web site for young mothers and aims to support young mothers of every kind.

Young Moms
www.youngmoms.org
The Young Mom web site provides support to young mothers and expecting mothers. The web site features poems, message boards and related resources.

Making Lemonade - Single Parent Support Group
www.makinglemonade.com
Making Lemonade is an on-line support system for the single parent. Web site features include forums, classified section, single parenting dating information and much more.

Parents Without Partners
www.parentswithoutpartners.org
This is the official web site for the organization devoted to the interests of single parents.

SAFER SEX AND BIRTH CONTROL

Depo-Provera
www.depo-provera.com
Commonly known as the "Birth Control Shot", Depo-Provera is birth control you only have to worry about 4 times a year.

Epigee-Birth Control Guide
www.epigee.org/guide
The Epigee birth control guide features information about

contraception currently available.

Reality-The Female Condom
www.femalehealth.com
The Female Health Company is the company that makes the Reality Female Condom, the first female condom on the market.

Mirena
www.mirena-us.com
Mirena is a long lasting birth control device that is placed in the uterus.

Ortho Evra
www.orthoevra.com
Ortho Evra is the first birth control patch on the market.

SEXUAL EDUCATION AND SUPPORT

Planned Parenthood
www.plannedparenthood.org
Planned parenthood.org is the official web site for the worlds largest reproductive health care organization. The web site features a wealth of information on a variety of topics.

Its Your Sex Life
www.itsyoursexlife.com
It's Your Sex Life aims to raise sexual awareness. Site features information on pregnancy, contraception, and sexually transmitted diseases.

Coalition For Positive Sexuality
www.positive.org
The goal of the Coalition For Positive Sexuality is to teach people positively about sexual education

Teenwire

www.teenwire.com

Teenwire provides sexuality and relationship information sponsored by The Planned Parenthood Federation of America.

TEEN PREGNANCY AND PREVENTION

National Campaign To End Teen Pregnancy

www.teenpregnancy.org

The goal of the National Campaign to Prevent Teen Pregnancy is to reduce the rate of teen pregnancy by one-third between 1996 and 2005. Site features resources, articles, quizzes, and tips for teens and parents.

CHAPTER 8 - Phone Numbers

AMT Children of Hope Foundation
   Infant Emergency Pick-Up Hotline
   1-877-796-4673

Lifetime Adoptions Birth Mother Hotline
   1-800-923-6784

Carnation Good Start Infant Formula
   1-800-248-8107

Crisis Pregnancy Hotline
   1-800-662-2678

Covenant House 9-Line
   1-800-999-999

Children Of The Night
   1-800-551-1331

Emergency Contraception Hotline
   1-888-not-2late

Enfamil Infant Formula
   1-800-baby-123

Food Stamp Hotline
  1-800-221-5689

Helpline
  1-888-467-8466

Mifeprex-Early Option Hotline
  1-877-432-7596

National Adoption Information Clearinghouse
  1-888-251-0075

National Network of Abortion Funds
  413-559-5645

Planned Parenthood
  1-800-230-plan

Project Cuddle 24-Hour Hotline
  1-888-628-3353

Birth Right Pregnancy Hotline
  1-800-550-4900

Similac
  1-800-227-5767

STD Info Line
  1-800-227-8922

Youth Crisis Hotline
  1-800-448-4663

WIC Hotline
  1-800-342-5942

CHAPTER 9 - Related Reading

ABORTION

Abortion-A Positive Decision
  Author Patricia Lunneborg
  Bergin & Garvey; ISBN: 0897892437; (May 1992)

The Abortion Resource Handbook
  Author K. Kaufmann
  Fireside, ISBN 0684830760 (July 1997)

The Choices We Made: Twenty Five Women and Me Speak Out About Abortion
  Authors Angela Bonavoglia (Editor), Gloria Steinem
  Publisher: Four Walls Eight Windows; ISBN: 1568581882; (March 30, 2001)

A Solitary Sorrow : Finding Healing & Wholeness After Abortion
  Authors Teri K. Reisser, Paul, Md. Reisser, pa Reisser
  Harold Shaw Pub; ISBN: 0877887748; (January 2000)

ADOPTION

The Adoption Resource Book
   Author Lois Gilman (Preface)
   Harper Reference; ISBN: 0062733613; 4th edition (November 1998)

The Complete Idiot's Guide to Adoption (Complete Idiot's Guides)
   Authors Christine A. Adamec, Chris Adamec, Chris Adamac, William Pierce
   MacMillan Distribution; ISBN: 0028621085; (January 1998)

The Essential Adoption Handbook
   Author Colleen Alexander-Roberts
   Taylor Pub; ISBN: 0878338403; (December 1993)

Children of Open Adoption and Their Families
   Author Kathleen Silber, Patricia Martinez Dorner
   Corona Pub; ISBN: 0931722780; (February 1990)

Dear Birth Mother
   Authors Kathleen Silber, Phylis Speedlin
   Corona Pub; ISBN: 0931722209; 3rd edition (December 1998)

The Open Adoption Experience: A Complete Guide for Adoptive and Birth Families--From Making the Decision Through the Child's Growing Years
   Authors Lois Ruskai Melina, Sharon Kaplan Roszia (Contributor)
   Harper Perennial; ISBN: 0060969571; (November 1993)

SINGLE PARENTING

The Single Parent Resource
   Authors Brook Noel, Arthur C. Klein, Art Klein (Contributor)

Champion Pr Ltd; ISBN: 1891400444; 1 edition (May 1998)

The Single Mother's Survival Guide
Authors Patrice Karst
Crossing Pr; ISBN: 1580910637; (March 2000)

*The Single Mother's Book : A Practical Guide to Managing Your
Children, Career, Home, Finances, and Everything Else*
Author Joan Anderson
Peachtree Publishers; ISBN: 0934601844; (July 1990)

The Complete Single Mother
Authors Andrea Engber, Leah Klungness
Adams Business Media; ISBN: 1580623026; 2nd edition (March 1, 2000)

On Our Own : Unmarried Motherhood in America
Author Melissa Ludtke
University of California Press; ISBN: 0520218302; (March 1999)

PREGNANCY

A Child Is Born
Author Lennart Nilsson
DTP; ISBN: 0440506913; Revised edition (May 1, 1986)

The Girlfriends Guide To Pregnancy
Author Vicki Iovine
Pocket Books; ISBN: 0671524313; (October 1995)

The Pregnancy Book
Authors Williams, Md. Sears, Martha Sears, William Sears, Linda
H. Holt
Little Brown & Co (Pap); ISBN: 0316779148; (June 1997)

While Waiting
Authors George E. Verrilli, Anne Marie Mueser, Marie Mueser (Contributor)
Griffin Trade Paperback; ISBN: 0312187750; 2nd Rev edition (June 1998)

The Mother of All Pregnancy Books
Author Ann Douglas
Hungry Minds, Inc; ISBN: 0764565168; 1st edition (January 1, 2002)

SEXUAL EDUCATION AND REPRODUCTIVE HEALTH

Smart Sex
Authors Jessica Vitkus, Marjorie Ingall, Jessica Weeks
Pocket Books, ISBN: 0671019104; (March 1998)

The Go Ask Alice Book of Answers: A Guide to Good Physical, Sexual, and Emotional Health
Author Columbia University's Health Education Program
Owl Books, ISBN: 0805055703; (September 1998)

About The Author

Dorrie Williams-Wheeler is an author, educator and web designer. She completed her Masters of Science of Education degree from Southern Illinois University. She has taught a variety of courses to adult learners. A former screenwriter, she penned the scripts *Keepin' It Real-A Hip Hop Love Story* and *Friendship Beyond Color Lines*. She is also the author of the book *Sparkledoll Always Into Something*. *The Unplanned Pregnancy Handbook* is her second book. She resides in Virginia Beach, Virginia with her husband and children. You can visit Dorrie on the web at www.dorrieinteractive.com.

REFERENCES

Brewer Sforza, Gail and Janice Presser Green. *Right From The Start.*
Emmaus: Rodale Press, 1981.

Erickson, Kristen. "Benefits of Breastfeeding." Today's Pregnancy, Birth Options Issue 2001: 7.

Fields, Denise, and Alan Fields. *Baby Bargains: Secrets to Saving 20% to 50% on Baby Furniture, Equipment, Clothes, Toys, Maternity Wear and Much, Much More!* New York: Windsor Peak Press, 2001.

Glasier A (1997). "Emergency postcoital contraception." New England Journal of Medicine, 337(15): 1058–1064.

Hamburg Copland, Jill. "Baby Bucks Money & More-Safe and Secure." Babytalk, March 2002: 64.

Huggins, Kathleen, R.N., M.S. *Nursing The First Two Months.* The Harvard Common Press, 1991.

Kuzemchak, Sally ; Jones, Sarah. "Birth Control Choices-A Roundup of What's New and What Works Best Post-Baby." American Baby May 2002: 61-65.

Link, David, M.D., Editor. *American Baby Guide To Parenting.* New York: Gallery Book, 1989.

Philadelphia Department of Public Health. *Healthy Foods, Healthy Baby.*
Philadelphia: Office of Maternal and Child Health. 1998.

Robinson, Bryan. "Delaware v. Grossberg and Peterson Grossberg To Serve Two-and-Half Years; Peterson Receives Two-Year Sentence." Court TV
Trials. 09071998. Court TV. 01052002. <http://www.courttv.com/trials/grossberg/070998.html.>

Rosen, Peg. "Beyond Baby Blues." American Baby May 2002: 95-100.

Saving Babies Together. Eating For Two. Wilkes-Barre: March of Dimes Birth Defects Foundation, 1998.

Spock, Benjamin,M.D., and Michael B. Rothenberg, M.D. *Dr. Spock's Baby and Child Care.* New York: Penguin Books, 1992.

Virginia Department of Health. *Why Every Woman Needs Folic Acid.* Richmond: 2001.

WEB REFERENCES

Abortion. Planned Parenthood of America. 4 April 2002. <http://www.plannedparenthood.org/ABORTION/>.

About Depo-Provera. Depo Provera. 22 March 2002. <http://www.depo-provera.com/consumer/about_depo/index.htm>.

ACLU Reproductive Rights: Mandatory Waiting Periods Before Abortions.   American Civil Liberties Union. 28 April 2002. <http://www.aclu.org/issues/reproduct/waiting_periods.html>.

Blood Typing-Test Overview.
Web MD. 1 April 2002.
<http://my.webmd.com/encyclopedia/article/4118.254>.

Choices for a Thereputic Abortion. Web MD. 1 May 2002
<http://my.webmd.com/encyclopedia/article/1840.53392>

Court TV On-Line New Jersey vs. Drexler. Court TV On-Line. 5 April 2002.
<http://www.courttv.com/trials/drexler/>.

Crisis Pregnancy Center of Tidewater. 1 May 2002.
<http://cpcot.org/>

Dilation and Evacuation (D&E) For Abortion. Web MD. 1, May 2002
<http://my.webmd.com/encyclopedia/article/1820.50530>

Family Medical Leave Act. National Adoption Information Clearing House. 15 May 2002.
<http://www.calib.com/naic/parents/fmla.htm>.

Food Stamp Program. U.S. Department of Agriculture. 23 April 2002
<http://www.fns.usda.gov/fsp/>.

Frequently Asked Questions-Is Depo-Provera a Good Choice For Most Women?
Depo-Provera Contraception Injection. 23 April 2002.
<http://www.depo-provera.com/consumer/about_depo/faq.htm>.

How Mifeprex Works. Mifeprex. 2 April 2002.
<http://www.mifeprex.com/how.php3>.

Induced Abortion U.S. The Alan Guttmacher Institute. 5 April 2002.
<http://www.cnn.com/US/9808/20/prom.birth.02/>.

Introduction to Adoption. National Adoption Information Clearing House. 3 May
2002. <http://www.calib.com/naic/parents/intro.htm>.

Just Another Girl On The I.R.T. All Movie Guide. 1 June 2002.
<http://ww.allmovie.com>.

Open Adoption. National Adoption Information Clearing House. 1 May 2002.
<http://www.calib.com/naic/pubs/f_openad.htm#what>.

Prom Mom Admits Killing Newborn. CNN.Com. 28 April 2002.
<http://www.cnn.com/US/9808/20/prom.birth.02/ >.

Routine Prenatal Tests. Kids Health For Parents. 2 April 2002.
<http://kidshealth.org/parent/system/medical/prenatal_tests_p4.html>.

Teen Sex and Pregnancy. The Alan Guttmacher Institute. 3 May 2002.
<http://www.agi-usa.org/pubs/fb_teen_sex.html>.

Saving Abandoned Newborns: Frequently Asked Questions About the Baby
Moses Project. The Baby Moses Project. 1 April 2002.
<http://www.babymoses.org/>.

What Is Mirena? Mirena USA. 28 April 2002.

<http://www.mirena-us.com/consumer/whatisframe.html>.

WIC At A Glance. U.S. Department of Agriculture. 8 April 2002
<http://www.fns.usda.gov/wic/ProgramInfo/WICataglance.htm>.

Vacuum Aspiration for Abortion Surgery Overview. Web MD. 1
May 2002.
<http://my.webmd.com/encyclopedia/article/
1840.53449#tw1081>

INDEX